A Mo
And A

Copyright © 2001 *by Kenette Molway*

Published by 21st Century Press
P.O. Box 8033
Springfield, MO 65801

ISBN 0-9700639-9-7

Illustrations: Steve Bjorkman
Cover and Book Design: IBIS Design: Lee Fredrickson

To: Grandma Maxine on Mothers Day 2001

From: Abigail & Brittany

Acknowledgements

A very special thanks to Steve Bjorkman. I had been praying for an illustrator, and God blessed me with my friend Steve. He is a world-renowned artist, and I never thought he could possibly find the time (with his own books, line of greeting cards, his own family and church involvement). Again, never underestimate the power of prayer. Steve said Yes! Steve is a true genius. His wit and talent can be seen on the cover and throughout this book. Steve, thanks again. Your art brought my words to life, and your work exceeded my greatest expectations. words cannot express my gratitude.

I thank God, who gave me my wonderful and loyal family. I want to say thank you to all of you, Gene, Holiday, Kyle, Tyler and Buddy, my sister and brother and their mates Kandi and Dave and Kenton and Laurie, and my Mom and Dad. And again, I thank God for all my encouraging friends. You know who you are and I love you...

Dedication

This book is dedicated to my steadfast mother who never stops walking and praying

Kenton, Kenette, Lois, Kenton and Kandi

Bright with anticipation, three little sets of eyes would peer through the radiant beam of sunlight. Every morning they awoke to this vision, the wonder of their Mommy on her knees before the holy God in the brilliant rays of the sun-because their Mommy loved the mornings best.

Why the anticipation? Because those three little children knew what was coming. Like the faithful rising of the sun, Mommy's prayers lifted up to the Father early in the morning every single day. First she would seek the touch of God on her own life. She would beseech the Lord: "God, please create in me the person you want me to be; without you I am nothing. Please give me the wisdom and strength to be a good wife and mother." Next she would pray earnestly for her God-given mate. Then, as three little pairs of ears listened, she would present at the throne of Almighty God her priceless treasures, her children.

And God Always Listened.

Finally, knowing as mothers somehow do, that her little cherubs were eagerly watching and waiting, she would jump up and say, "Good morning! This is the day that the Lord has made! Rejoice and be glad in it!" With a swift hug for each giggling child, she would proclaim, "I love you!" and ask, "How can I pray for you today?" Eyes wide with sincerity, the three would ask, "Mommy, do your prayers do any good?" She would respond, "Do my prayers do any good? They most certainly do! That's why I pray and pray and pray, just for you."

Mommy's faith was strong and convincing, and by breakfast time the children would eagerly share their many requests. Then, assured that their needs were in good hands, they would skip off to play the day away while Mommy prayed.

And God always listened.

As the seasons passed, the children grew and eventually went to school. Then Mommy began to pray by the block! Each precious child got one whole, long block, as Mommy walked before the Lord to intercede for her family. To the south was Kenton's block. Past the blue house and around the corner, and there was Kenette's block. Up the little hill and past the big oak tree, Mommy would begin to walk Kandi's block.

Mommy would pray, as promised, for things like caterpillars and the adopted bird with a broken wing-and for the monsters

under the bed to go away. And, of course, there was the ham-ster that wasn't feeling very well, having failed his audition as an Indy- 500 racecar. Step by dedicated step, Mommy would pray for the safety of her children, and she would pray for angels to surround and protect each of them. As asked, she would pray for the kitties that ran away and for His healing of the puppy that couldn't fly after all. She would humbly ask God to give each of her children wisdom to make godly deci-sions, to choose good friends, and to live no wasted years.

She would ask God to keep each child in the palm of His almighty hand. Her work yet unfinished, Mommy would then add more blocks and pray for best friends and children she didn't even know yet, the future mates of her own children.

And God always listened.

Faithful through the years, Mommy continued her vigil. Every day she would kneel before the Lord in the early morning, because Mommy loved mornings best. And she would greet her children with her cheerful quotation: "Good morning! This is the day that the Lord has made! Rejoice and be glad in it!" Then she would give them a loving squeeze and say, "I love you! How can I pray for you today?" Still her youngsters would ask, "Mommy, do your prayers do any good?" As always, Mommy would assure them, "They most certainly do! That's why I pray and pray and I pray, just for you."

As her children grew and matured, their prayer requests also grew and matured. Their breakfast-table requests had grown to include important matters like the changing of mean teachers into nice teachers, for good luck at musical recitals and games, for new bikes, and relief from playground bullies. Around the blocks Mommy would deliberately march, praying as she went.

And God always listened.

In no time at all, the one-time toddlers became TEENAGERS! Greeted with their mother's morning rally in her perky and happy voice, "Good morning! This is the day that the Lord has made! Rejoice and be glad in it," they would tic and hiss, growl, and roll over, "begging" that she go away. Undaunted, Mommy, now "Mom," would declare, "I love you! How can I pray for you today?" Mom may have loved mornings best, but her teenagers did not! Sometimes they would toss pillows at her and plead, "Please, Mom, let us sleep. God isn't even up yet. This early in the morning your prayers can't possibly do any good!" Mom would respond with vigor, "God never sleeps, and He always listens. Of course my prayers do good; they most certainly do. That's why I pray and pray and I pray just for you." Knowing that their Mom would not go away, the teens would sarcastically tell their Mom to pray for a new mother for them, one who would not wake them with such a perky and happy voice, asking them for prayer requests.

Still, Mom never stopped walking and praying. Not always certain how to handle three active, independent teens, she added more blocks to her prayer regimen. The neighborhood was hers, consecrated as a prayer path. She would intercede for them, as her adolescents encountered the unique pressures and turmoil of their generation. Sensing their need, she would spend even more hours on her knees in prayer for them. She wore out her knees seeking wisdom for herself and for her husband, and she fervently kept praying for her teenagers, even through hard times and poor choices.

And God always listened.

By and by, the storms of the teen years were weathered, and the children went off to college. Still their Mom remained faithful in her morning prayers-because she loved mornings best. Her heart full of love, she would phone her children each week and remind them, "I love you! How can I pray for you today?" Since the faithful prayers of their godly mother had educated them, her young adults willingly shared their requests: "Mom, please pray for our classes and that we get

good grades on our finals." They would ask prayer for special boyfriends and girlfriends. As their spiritual maturity began to unfold, each child would add, "Mom, please pray that God will keep me in the palm of His almighty hand. And, Mom, thanks; I love you, too." Then, of course, their Mom would hang up the phone, to walk and pray.

And God always listened.

Eventually, in answer to their mother's prayers, each child chose wisely in selecting a mate. One by one, as Mom met each fiancé for the first time, she would say, "So you're the one I've been praying for all these years!" And then, God awarded her with a mother's most awesome miracle, grandchildren! When she met each new grandchild, she would say, "Hello, God's Little Gift, I'm going to pray for you every morning" because Mom, now "Grandma" loved mornings best.

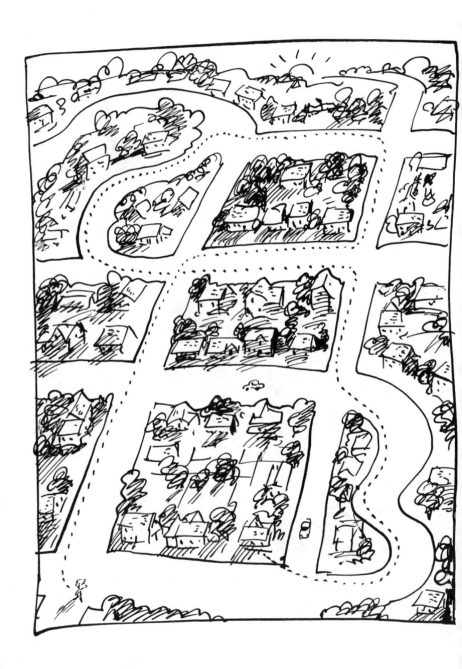

Adding to her prayer blocks, she would present each blessed little child to God for his safekeeping. When her grandchildren were old enough to talk, she would tell them, "I love you!" and ask, "How can I pray for you today?"

She then took each little toddler on a tour of his or her own special block, showing them where she walked and prayed just for that little soul. She prayed for wisdom and no wasted years for them. She always prayed that God would keep them in the palm of His almighty hand.

And God always listened.

This Grandma never missed one of her grandchildren's games, track meets, recitals, or programs. She was their biggest fan and she always clapped and cheered the loudest. And even while she was cheering and clapping, Grandma was praying that each of her beloved grandchildren would always do his or her best.

And God always listened.

As the years rolled by, the morning sun would always find Grandma on her knees before the Lord, praying for her children, who were now raising TEENAGERS of their own. Then, with her walking shoes on, ready to do battle, she would call her children one by one and say, "I love you! How can I pray for you today?" Now dedicated fans of their praying mother, each grown child would blurt out, "Oh, Mom, I was just on my knees praying for my kids. It's so hard to raise TEENAGERS! Do you think my prayers are doing any good? Please pray with me." And she would encourage her frazzled children, "You know by now all the good our prayers do. That's why I pray and pray and I pray just for you."

Then Grandma would set off to walk and pray. She had worn out her knees and nearly walked out a groove in the neighborhood pavement praying for her own children, but she kept on praying. She prayed that her teenaged grandchildren would have wisdom, make good friends, live no wasted years, and remain in the palm of His almighty hand.

And God always listened.

Early in the morning although it's been many years, Grandma still paces the blocks and prays. Whether the sun shines or the rain pelts, each darling grandchild can watch their grandma walking as they drive to school, and each one knows which is his or her block and can proudly say, "She's praying for me!"

Now, as I kneel in the warmth of the morning sun, I thank God that this amazing mother is my mother. Because of her, my brother and sister and I with all our precious children know that we are loved and prayed for.

And that God always listens.